States

HAWAII

by Angie Swanson

CAPSTONE PRESS
a capstone imprint

Next Page Books are published by Capstone Press,
1710 Roe Crest Drive, North Mankato, Minnesota 56003
www.mycapstone.com

Library of Congress Cataloging-in-Publication Data
Cataloging-in-publication information is on file with the Library of
Congress.
ISBN 978-1-5157-0397-6 (library binding)
ISBN 978-1-5157-0457-7 (paperback)
ISBN 978-1-5157-0509-3 (ebook PDF)

Editorial Credits
Jaclyn Jaycox, editor; Richard Korab and Katy LaVigne, designers;
Morgan Walters, media researcher; Laura Manthe, production specialist

Photo Credits
Capstone Press: Angi Gahler, map 4, 7; CriaImages.com: Jay Robert
Nash Collection, top 19; Getty Images: De Agostini Picture Library,
12, Lucy Pemoni / Stringer, middle 19, Paul Conklin, bottom 18;
iStockphoto: mychadre77, middle left 21; Library of Congress: Pete
Souza, bottom 19; Newscom: Kyodo, top 18, Laura Farr/ZUMA Press,
middle 18; North Wind Picture Archives, 26; One Mile Up, Inc.,
22–23; Shutterstock: AHPix, bottom left 20, Alexey Kamenskiy, 7,
top 24, Andrew Zarivny, 11, bikeriderlondon, bottom 21, Boykov,
bottom right 20, Darren J. Bradley, middle right 21, Deborah Kolb,
17, EpicStockMedia, bottom right 8, top right 21, Ethan Daniels,
top left 21, Everett Collection, 29, Galyna Andrushko, 5, Hywit
Dimyadi, bottom 24, KimPinPhotography, top right 20, kshiota, top
left 20, Maridav, bottom left 8, 14, mj007, 13, Paul B. Moore, 27,
Paul Laubach, 9, Pierre Leclerc, 6, Sarah Fields Photography, cover,
Shoriful Chowdhury, 15, tomas del amo, 16, vasen, 25, Wildnerdpix, 10;
Wikimedia: MSGT STEPHEN B. JONES "Released to Public," 28

All design elements by Shutterstock

Printed and bound in China.
0316/CA21600187
012016   009436F16

TABLE OF CONTENTS

Want to take your research further? Ask your librarian if your school subscribes to PebbleGo Next. If so, when you see this helpful symbol 🔺 throughout the book, log onto www.pebblegonext.com for bonus downloads and information.

LOCATION

Hawaii is a long string of islands in the middle of the Pacific Ocean. Hawaii is made up of 132 islands. These islands are the tops of ancient, undersea volcanoes. As the volcanoes erupted, lava built up to reach above sea level. Hawaii is the only state that's not part of North America. Hawaii is 2,000 miles (3,219 kilometers) southwest of California. Hawaii stretches across a vast area of the ocean. Still, its total land area is small. Only three other states are smaller—Connecticut, Delaware, and Rhode Island. Hawaii's capital and biggest city is Honolulu. Honolulu is on the island Oahu. Hawaii's other large cities are Hilo, Kailua, and Kaneohe.

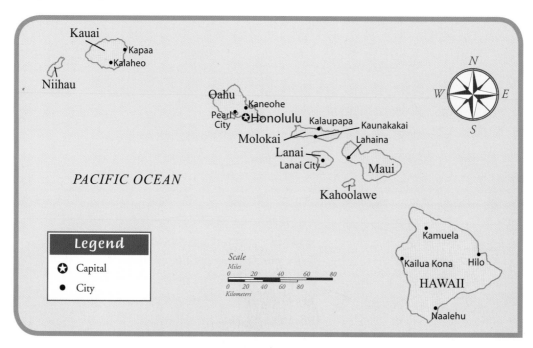

PebbleGo Next Bonus! To print and label your own map, go to www.pebblegonext.com and search keywords:

HI MAP

Honolulu is surrounded by over 100 beaches, more than almost any other city in the world.

GEOGRAPHY

Shoreline makes up one-sixth of Hawaii's land. Most of the land is at sea level, but some parts rise to great heights. Tall cliffs are found on some areas of the coast. Waterfalls flow over the cliffs into the ocean. The active volcano Mauna Loa is 13,680 feet (4,170 meters) high. Mauna Kea is Hawaii's highest peak. It stands 13,796 feet (4,205 m) tall. Tropical forests grow on Hawaii's larger islands. Most of Hawaii's islands have white sand beaches. Black sand covers other beaches.

PebbleGo Next Bonus! To watch a video about the Big Island's volcanic activity, go to www.pebblegonext.com and search keywords:

HI VIDEO

Many tourists take helicopter tours to view the beautiful island coasts from above.

The summit of Mauna Kea marks the highest elevation in Hawaii.

Kawaikini Peak
Mount Waialeale
Niihau
Kauai

PACIFIC OCEAN

Oahu

Kalaupapa National Historical Park

Molokai

Lanai Maui

Haleakala National Park

Kahoolawe

Mauna Kea

Hawaii

Wailuku River

Hualalai Volcano

Mauna Loa

Kilauea Volcano

Hawaii Volcanoes National Park

Legend

▲ Highest Point

⛰ Mountain Range

■ National Park

〰 River

🌋 Volcano

Scale
Miles
0   20   40   60   80
0   20   40   60   80
Kilometers

WEATHER

Hawaii has a tropical climate. Hawaii's temperatures are warm for much of the year. The average January temperature is 68 degrees Fahrenheit (20 degrees Celsius). The average July temperature is 75°F (24°C).

Average High and Low Temperatures (Honolulu, HI)

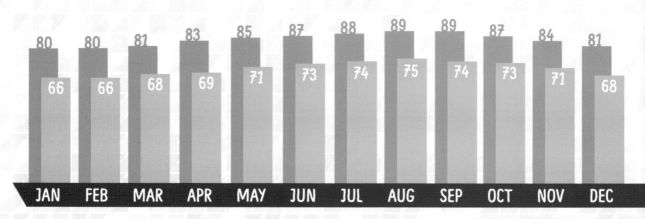

	JAN	FEB	MAR	APR	MAY	JUN	JUL	AUG	SEP	OCT	NOV	DEC
High	80	80	81	83	85	87	88	89	89	87	84	81
Low	66	66	68	69	71	73	74	75	74	73	71	68

LANDMARKS

Waikiki Beach

Waikiki Beach is a popular beach on Oahu's south shore. Tourists swim, surf, and canoe in the deep blue ocean waters.

Mauna Loa

Mauna Loa is the world's largest volcano. Found on the island of Hawaii, Mauna Loa is 13,680 feet (4,170 m) high. It is one of the most active volcanoes. Mauna Loa has erupted 33 times since 1843. Its most recent eruption was in 1984.

USS *Arizona* Memorial

In 1941 Japanese bombers sank the USS *Arizona* battleship during their attack on Pearl Harbor on the island of Oahu. The USS *Arizona* Memorial is built on top of the sunken battleship. A memorial museum offers films and exhibits about the event.

HISTORY AND GOVERNMENT

Explorer Captain Cook sailed to Hawaii in 1778. He named the archipelago the "Sandwich Islands."

Between AD 200 and 600, Polynesians became the first people to settle on Hawaii. Around AD 1000, the first Tahitians came to the islands. They are thought to be Hawaii's natives. British Captain James Cook became the first white explorer to land on Hawaii in 1778. In 1810 King Kamehameha became the first leader to join the islands under one rule. In 1894 the Republic of Hawaii was created by a small group of Americans, Europeans, and their followers. Hawaii became a U.S. territory in 1900. Hawaii became the 50th state in 1959.

Hawaii's state government has three branches. The governor is the leader of the executive branch. The legislature is made up of the 25-member Senate and the 51-member House of Representatives. They make the laws for Hawaii. Hawaii's judges and courts are the judicial branch. They uphold the laws.

Hawaii's state capitol building is located in Honolulu.

INDUSTRY

Tourism is Hawaii's largest industry. Millions of tourists visit Hawaii each year. They spend money in restaurants, hotels, and shops. More than nine out of 10 workers in Hawaii hold service jobs. No other state relies so heavily on services.

Farmland covers about 25 percent of Hawaii's land. Sugarcane and pineapple are Hawaii's main crops. Hawaii's other major farm products include livestock, coffee, tropical plants, macadamia nuts, taro, and kava. Fishing is another important industry. Tuna and swordfish are the major catches.

Hawaii's beauty and tropical location make it a top tourist destination.

Food products are Hawaii's leading factory goods. Some food plants turn sugarcane into sugar and molasses. Others process pineapples and other fruit. They make canned fruit, fruit juice, and jelly.

Sugarcane stalks can grow as high as 20 feet (6 m) tall.

POPULATION

Hawaii is one of the most diverse states in the nation. Asians are Hawaii's largest ethnic group. Many Asians have Japanese roots. Others are Chinese, Filipino, or Korean. White people are Hawaii's second-largest ethnic group. Most white people came from the U.S. mainland. Hawaii's third-largest group is made up of those with mixed ethnicity. These residents are a combination of two or more races. Lifelong residents of Hawaii call themselves *kamaaina*. They usually use the term *Hawaiians* for native Hawaiians. Many native speakers of the Hawaiian language live on the Molokai and Niihau islands.

Population by Ethnicity

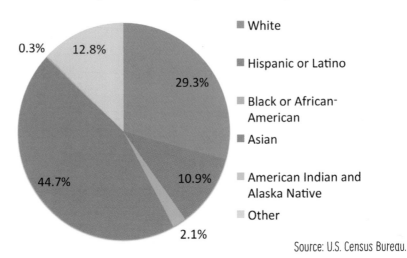

- 0.3%
- 12.8%
- 29.3%
- 44.7%
- 10.9%
- 2.1%

- White
- Hispanic or Latino
- Black or African-American
- Asian
- American Indian and Alaska Native
- Other

Source: U.S. Census Bureau.

FAMOUS PEOPLE

George Ariyoshi (1926–) was a governor of Hawaii (1974–1986) and the first Japanese-American governor of a U.S. state. He was born in Honolulu.

Angela Perez Baraquio (1976–) was Miss America 2001. She is the first Asian-American and the first teacher to become Miss America. She was born in Honolulu.

Hiram Fong (1906–2004) was Hawaii's first Chinese-American to serve in the U.S. Senate (1959–1977). He was also the first Asian-American in the Senate. He was born on the island of Oahu.

Kamehameha I (circa 1758–1819) was the first king of Hawaii. He united most of Hawaii into one kingdom. He was born on the island of Hawaii.

Don Ho (1930–2007) was a singer who made Hawaiian music widely popular. His biggest hit was *Tiny Bubbles* (1966). He was born in Honolulu.

Barack Obama (1961–) was elected president of the United States in 2008. He was re-elected in 2012. Obama represented Illinois in the U.S. Senate from 2005 to 2008. He was born in Honolulu.

STATE SYMBOLS

Tree

candlenut

Flower

yellow hibiscus

Bird

nene (Hawaiian goose)

Dance

hula

PebbleGo Next Bonus! To make a traditional Hawaiian dessert, go to www.pebblegonext.com and search keywords:

HI RECIPE

Marine Animal

humpback whale

Individual Sport

surfing

Gem

black coral

Fish

rectangular triggerfish

Team Sport

outrigger canoe paddling

FAST FACTS

STATEHOOD
1959

CAPITAL
Honolulu

LARGEST CITY •
Honolulu

SIZE
6,423 square miles (16,635 square kilometers) land area (2010 U.S. Census Bureau)

POPULATION
1,404,054 (2013 U.S. Census estimate)

STATE NICKNAME
Aloha State

STATE MOTTO
"The Life of the Land is Perpetuated in Righteousness"

STATE SEAL

The state seal has a shield in the center. Above the shield is the date 1959, the year Hawaii became a state. A figure of King Kamehameha I is on one side of the shield. The Goddess of Liberty holding the Hawaiian flag is on the other side. Below the shield is a bird called a phoenix. The phoenix is surrounded by leaves of native plants—the taro, banana, and maidenhair fern. Around the border is the state motto in the Hawaiian language.

PebbleGo Next Bonus!
To print and color
your own flag, go to
www.pebblegonext.com
and search keywords:
HI FLAG

STATE FLAG

Hawaii's state flag is red, white, and blue. It was designed in the early 1800s. The flag's eight stripes stand for Hawaii's eight major islands. The upper left corner is the Union Jack, the flag of Great Britain. King Kamehameha I, who ruled the Hawaiian Islands from 1810 to 1819, had a strong friendship with Great Britain.

MINING PRODUCTS

gemstones, limestone, sand and gravel, traprock

MANUFACTURED GOODS

petroleum and coal products, food products, transportation equipment, printed material, furniture, plastic and rubber products

FARM PRODUCTS

sugarcane, pineapples, macadamia nuts, coffee, flowers

PebbleGo Next Bonus!
To learn the lyrics to
the state song, go to
www.pebblegonext.com
and search keywords:

HI SONG

HAWAII TIMELINE

1620 — The Pilgrims establish a colony in the New World in present-day Massachusetts.

1778 — Captain James Cook of the British Navy lands in Hawaii. He is the first white explorer to arrive in Hawaii.

1810 — King Kamehameha becomes the first leader to unite the islands under one ruler.

1820 — The first American missionaries bring Christianity to Hawaii.

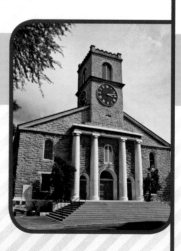

1835 Hawaii's first permanent sugar plantation opens on Kauai Island.

1840 The Kingdom of Hawaii adopts its first constitution.

1861–1865 The Union and the Confederacy fight the Civil War.

1893 The Hawaiian monarchy is overthrown on January 17 in a revolution led by nine Americans and four Europeans.

1894 The Republic of Hawaii is established. Sanford B. Dole, a judge, is elected president of the republic.

1900 Hawaii becomes a U.S. territory. All residents of Hawaii are now American citizens.

1908 Pearl Harbor on Oahu becomes a U.S. naval station.

1914–1918 World War I is fought; the United States enters the war in 1917.

1927 U.S. Army lieutenants A. F. Hegenberger and L. J. Maitland make the first airplane flight between the U.S. mainland and Hawaii.

1939–1945 World War II is fought; the United States enters the war in 1941.

1941 The Japanese attack Pearl Harbor on the island of Oahu on December 7. The attack brings the United States into World War II.

1959 Hawaii becomes the 50th U.S. state on August 21.

1986 John Waihee is elected Hawaii's first native Hawaiian governor.

1992 Hurricane Iniki hits Hawaii, killing four people and causing more than $2 billion in damages. The island of Kauai suffers the most damage. Many of its homes and businesses are destroyed.

2002 Linda Lingle becomes the first woman to be elected governor of Hawaii. She is re-elected in 2006.

2008 Hawaii native Barack Obama is elected the 44th U.S. president.

2013 Hilo's Merrie Monarch Festival, celebrating Hawaiian culture and hula dancing, marks its 50th anniversary.

2015 The Solar Impulse lands in Hawaii after completing the longest flight for a solar-powered aircraft in history.

Glossary

archipelago *(ar-kuh-PE-luh-goh)*—a group of small islands

culture *(KUHL-chuhr)*—a group of people's beliefs, customs, and way of life

eruption *(i-RUHP-shuhn)*—the action of throwing out rock, hot ash, and lava from a volcano with great force

executive *(ig-ZE-kyuh-tiv)*—the branch of government that makes sure laws are followed

industry *(IN-duh-stree)*—a business which produces a product or provides a service

legislature *(LEJ-iss-lay-chur)*—a group of elected officials who have the power to make or change laws for a country or state

petroleum *(puh-TROH-lee-uhm)*—an oily liquid found below the earth's surface used to make gasoline, heating oil, and many other products

plantation *(plan-TAY-shuhn)*—a large farm found in warm climates where crops such as coffee, tea, rubber, and cotton are grown

resident *(REZ-uh-duhnt)*—someone who lives in a particular place

revolution *(rev-uh-LOO-shun)*—an uprising by a group of people against a system of government or a way of life

Read More

Otfinoski, Steven. *Hawaii: The Aloha State.* It's My State! New York: Cavendish Square Publishing, 2016.

Ganeri, Anita. *United States of America: A Benjamin Blog and His Inquisitive Dog Guide.* Country Guides. Chicago: Heinemann Raintree, 2015.

Meinking, Mary. *What's Great About Hawaii?* Our Great States. Minneapolis: Lerner Publications, 2015.

Internet Sites

FactHound offers a safe, fun way to find Internet sites related to this book. All of the sites on FactHound have been researched by our staff.

Here's all you do:

Visit *www.facthound.com*

Type in this code: 9781515703976

Check out projects, games and lots more at
www.capstonekids.com

Critical Thinking Using the Common Core

1. Found on the island of Hawaii, Mauna Loa is the world's largest volcano. It is also one of the most active volcanoes. When was the last time it erupted? (Key Ideas and Details)

2. In 1941 the Japanese attacked Pearl Harbor on the island of Oahu. The attack brought the United States into World War II. Do you think the United States would have stayed out of World War II if Pearl Harbor had not been attacked? Why or why not? (Integration of Knowledge and Ideas)

3. Hawaii is one of the most diverse states in the nations. Looking at the pie chart on page 16, what are its three largest ethnic groups? (Key Ideas and Details)

Index